Once upon a time in New York City

Hideaki Sato
Japan Professional Photographers' Association

Born in 1943 in Niigata, Japan, Sato majored in photography at the prestigious Nihon University, and soon embarked on a career as a freelance photographer. Fascinated by nature, lifestyles and culture, he traveled the world extensively photographing people and places from locations as varied as the Arctic, Alaska, mainland US, Africa and Tibet. His first trip to New York City in 1967 was to start a love affair with the city that has lasted for more than 30 years.

Highly acclaimed published works in Japan include "100 Miles to the Sea," "Town at the End of the Earth," "This is How I Became a Photographer," and "Rain Has Many Names". He has also held periodic photo exhibitions in Japan from 1989.

REQUIEM WORLD TRADE CENTER
Once upon a time in New York City

Photographer : Hideaki Sato
Art director : Toshiaki Ichikawa (Office Ichikawa)
　　　　　　Tokuji Katagiri (Toho-shoin)
Editorial director : Holy Gomen

Published by ICG Muse, Inc.
5-10-33 Roppongi, Minato-ku, Tokyo 106-0032.

Originally Published in 2001 by Magazine Support, Co. Ltd., Tokyo.

All rights reserved. Printed in Singapore.

ISBN4-925080-71-7

REQUIEM
WORLD TRADE CENTER

Once upon a time in New York City

HIDEAKI SATO

ICG MUSE

THE TOWERS UNTOLD

A photographer's New York City, before the fall.

We all saw the video. A black wave whips around the corner of a building and races furiously toward the camera — the wave itself as tall as a tall building. It flows like water but lands like stone, and it sucks the air and light out of everything in its path. History is like that cruel wave. Tales told in a thousand languages cohere in a single chorus, which pours over us. The ringing that remains in our ears, the chorus declares, will never stop and never change. The tale is told, what is cannot be undone. Now we know the tale of the towers, the story of September. We knew, when we saw the black wave, what it was made of.

In the mid-sixties a young Japanese man came to New York. If an artist is always coming into being, he was at the very start of that cycle. Photography was already a constant for him, but he sought a larger tableau of sights, sounds and experience to set his eye and hand to. Pulling up stakes for New York was not then commonplace among young Japanese men. Certainly many did, but often as not on a dare. He was at the edge of the world to that moment, drawing the map as he traveled.

He photographed madly, testing approaches, flirting with theory. But you don't see in these photographs the mighty hunter and his trophy. You see a soul timorously working its way out the aperture of the eye to search the frame. Amid a city where self-expression needs no coaxing, you hear questions of self and identity. You feel equal measures of fear and optimism, conflict and hope. You sense, because he is dealing with his own hurdles of language and culture, that the camera serves not so much to capture time forever as to soften the impertinence of the artist's stare.

In the faces of police officers the artist sees an understanding of personal responsibility not definable on familiar terms. The enthusiasm of protestors speaks of conviction and idealism. The poor, the isolated, the disenfranchised all carry themselves with the determined posture of survivors. Personal responsibility, conviction, strength and survival; how did the young artist know that those themes would adhere to this story forever?

Two years on, just as unease and homesickness rapidly advance on him, the photographer's attention is commanded by a project of otherworldly size. All of the momentum and energy that ignites this city is channeled into this singular promise of the future. Its presentation is stark and fearless. Its mass begins to thrust upward before his eyes in a gesture of exaltation. This was the World Trade Center as the embodiment of life being lived, before it was a workplace, and a legend, and ultimately a martyr. This was sheer exuberance annealing into form before the photographer's eyes.

Autumn, 2001. Fall brings with it a reason for the artist to see through these eyes again.

Autumn should be met with open arms, because it is eternal. In spring we gather all the experience we can. In summer we draw our conclusions and act on them. In autumn there is finally time to learn from our striving, and distance enough from the earlier self, that forgiveness and understanding are possible. Autumn offers the greatest promise for what was so elusive in earlier seasons: Truth, tempered in fire, stronger than steel. If autumn is approached properly, winter will be endurable.

David G. Imber, Editor

Once upon a time in New York City   Hideaki Sato

Destroyed by the terrorist attacks of September 11, the World Trade Center was a virtuosic architectural symbol which I admired and photographed for more than 30 years. It captured my imagination and I can honestly say that, as a subject, it served as my initiation into the photographic industry. I photographed the magnificent skyscrapers from before their inception to well after their completion; and after my long, personal relationship with the buildings, the final nightmarish scene of the towers collapsing was especially heart wrenching. My pain, of course, cannot be compared in even the smallest sense, to that of the victims and their families of this terrible tragedy. Because of this, I pray that my photographs can somehow support those in need at this time.

My first introduction to the WTC was in 1967 when I had just graduated from college with a degree in photography. I decided to move to New York City in order to hone my craft. That was a special time in Japan because it was newly possible for many Japanese to go abroad and explore the world. Many of my friends, like myself, left Japan to follow their dreams.

Soon after my arrival at New York, I was sure that I made the right decision. Just within an hour or so after I got off the bus from Los Angeles, I was overwhelmed by the diversity of people there and energy on the streets. Everything I had longed to capture with my camera was sprinkled all over the city, it seemed.

Like most newly arrived visitors, I found myself living in a cheap studio apartment on the lower West Side. During the day I would walk the streets of New York shooting as many pictures as I could. I particularly enjoyed wandering through the downtown area trying to capture details of the residents' "everyday" life. I often walked through the West Village to Washington Square where two or three hours would disappear as I photographed the street performers. On my weekend shoots I never seemed to have enough rolls of film to capture the excitement of this area.

From there, I would walk along 4th Street to 2nd Avenue, where the streets were filled with every kind of imaginable character and my photographs were as varied as the humanity I met along the way. Heading south from Houston Street, I would walk down Orchard Street to the Bowery. At that time this was a less than desirable neighborhood to spend any time in, and on more than one occasion, I had to make a speedy getaway from a subject that didn't appreciate my presence. This was a very thrilling time for me, despite some danger, and was an exciting contrast to the more homogenous nature of my homeland.

It was around this time that many older buildings in lower Manhattan were being demolished in preparation for the World Trade Center. Some of the grand old facades of the area remained but many were slowly giving way to make room for buildings of a new era. When I felt like I might collapse from exhaustion, I somehow used to manage to find my way over to the WTC construction site. The scale of this project was so immense that I found my fatigue soon replaced with a strong desire to photograph this phenomenal undertaking. While I couldn't tell what the 100-storey plus towers would ultimately look like, I could plainly see that something enormous and record-breaking was in the making. The size of the space created when all of the old buildings were finally cleared was truly impressive. Three buildings on the periphery of the site survived and in one of them a bar remained opened until the construction began on the towers. This bar was like an oasis to me and I would often enjoy a few cold beers there after a long day in the field. I remember one day in particular when I exited the bar, feeling a bit tipsy, and looking out onto the massive construction site. I stood in awe as a peered across the vacant site at the lights of the many skyscrapers as they glowed in the night like a Milky Way planted in the middle of the metropolis.

Just as the site was cleared and work began on the foundation, a dream job came my way and I left New York for a while. In the following months I had the great pleasure to cover the Apollo 11 mission to the moon. For a young Japanese photographer to witness in person what millions of people around the world were watching on their televisions was a bewildering honor. At the end of the remarkable assignment though I made my way directly back to New York City.

When I arrived I found that the site had been hollowed out in preparation for the huge supports required to stabilize the towers. The workers were busy at the very bottom of the deep hole diligently digging and carrying the dislodged rocks to the surface for removal. Before long the steel structure began stretching skywards on the North Tower. I had just bought a bellows camera from a friend and as the WTC started taking shape, this was a perfect opportunity to practice on my new gadget. As construction intensified, I gained even more confidence by shooting the workers and onlookers with my new 35mm camera.

Once the skeletal frames were completed, the towers went up at breakneck speed. At that time I was captivated by the sheer enormity of the walls of the complex as well as the intensity on the faces of the workers. Before leaving Japan, I had marveled at the size of the recently completed Kasumigaseki building in Tokyo. But the American accomplishment towered dramatically over the Japanese landmark.

The size difference in these two buildings seemed to reflect the relative difference in the economic might of the two countries.

In the fall of 1969 I sadly left New York without the thrill of seeing the towers completed. Never in my wildest thoughts could I have imagined the World Trade Center coming to such a tragic demise. As I look at my photos now, they seem to me to be a humble diary of the life of the buildings as well as of my own life. They spark many warm memories of the WTC and the people of New York City.

In the years after 1969, I always sought out jobs that would take me back to New York and allow me to continue my lifework. Those later pictures often focus on the characters of this vibrant city. I would walk endlessly from one end of the island to the other in search of interesting subjects. But whether one was walking around downtown or coming up out of a subway in midtown, somehow and somewhere the WTC made its presence known. For me, there was no more important landmark in New York City. When I look at the old photos I shot from a Staten Island bound ferry before the WTC was constructed, I am filled with nostalgia about the architectural marvel that would soon dominate that skyline. But now, 30 years later, that same skyline leaves me with a strange void in my heart.

When I saw the towers collapse on that clear autumn morning, I knew then that I would soon return to the site that taught me so much about my craft and my life. I would go back to pay homage to the many souls who were lost that day, as well as to the souls responsible for the WTC's creation. In publishing this book, I pray for all of those whose lives were sacrificed and for the many rescue workers who bravely gave their own lives while trying to save others. In a strange twist of fate, I will once again look across the same vacant site at an unclear future. In such complicated times, the mighty efforts of these heroic New Yorkers are an inspiration to the rest of the world.

There is hope　　　　　*Hideaki Sato*

From the ferry's cabin, a young boy gazes at New York Harbor.

Veteran ferry-goers, on their way. Spring 1967.

Bound for Staten Island. Lower Manhattan recedes in the mist. Circa 1967.

Off the ferry and on to work.

This is where the World Trade Center will be built.

Cobblestones and cars, all will vanish.

At the nearby subway entrance a passerby notices the commotion, assays the cityscape for subtle changes.

From weeds and discarded buildings, the land will soon teem with life. Autumn 1967.

The local infrastructure will undergo complete renewal. Autumn 1967.

The startling vastness of the area being cleared for construction. Autumn 1967.

To the left, the waterfront. 1.2 million cubic yards of earth and rock cleared from the site will form an entirely new one.

Barricades are erected around the site as construction begins. Autumn 1967.

The debris of old buildings, carted out on flatbed trucks. Autumn 1967.

A scrap heap of demolished buildings waiting to be cleared. Winter 1967.

Dusk blankets the expanse of the construction site.

The construction site is finally cleared. Serenity will soon give way to frenetic activity. Winter 1967.

 I was fascinated by the old methods of demolition. This huge lead object was swung against buildings to bring them down.

The anticipation of change was palpable and vivid. Winter 1967.

Breathing in a vista on the verge of redesign. A quiet Sunday morning in Queens. Winter 1967.

The L train on 14th street. I traveled this line a lot to visit a fellow I befriended named Russ Hoffman. He later became a police officer. Winter 1967.

Stranger in a Times Square snack bar, New Year's Eve, 1967. The outfit and salute a mystery, the sentiment perfectly clear.

A ferry stalwart, Staten Island bound. Emergent buildings begin to alter the background geometry. Winter 1967.

The ferry port at the foot of the new skyline. The varieties of ferry were distinguishable by their tail portions. Spring 1968.

An old Wall Street tavern. A bit too upscale for me to have frequented. Winter 1968.

There were ancient holdouts among both the bars that dotted the surrounding neighborhood and their denizens.

Massive stretches of earth are exposed as the World Trade Center site begins to take shape. Spring 1968.

Spring snow, 1968.

Construction underway. The shops carried on without missing a beat, some to this day. Spring 1968.

There was no question of whose domain the site was. Their movements expressed authority and devotion to this place. That mysterious New York "pride of place" appeared equally in those who lived and worked there.

Workers take a short break on Liberty street. I grew to greatly admire these men...

...who assumed the stature of giants, even in repose. Spring 1968.

Firefighters at a parade. Spring 1968.

The marchers and the spectators. The bond of commitment and security.

Street nameplates were removed by "collectors". A city that belonged to its people, taken literally. Spring 1968.

Viewing holes around the construction site. Spring 1968.

The factory and warehouse district on West 34th street. Another artifact of an earlier Manhattan culture. Spring 1968.

A day at the races. These people all turned out to watch legendary jockey Willie Shoemaker.

Jazz great Sun Ra and his musicians broke into an impromptu performance one day on the ferry.

A Korean street performer. The street was theatre then, and its energy flowed unbounded into every public space. Spring 1968.

From this stage, the building rose at record speed. Spring 1968.

The rationale behind the different underground floor heights was impenetrable. I find this sort of thing endlessly fascinating. Summer 1968.

The depth of the support intimated a height that was hard to imagine. Summer 1968.

An assembly point on a prefabricated steel frame portion.

The mathematical precision of the framed tube structure is starkly evident in this early view.

An understated herald for a breathtakingly ambitious enterprise. Summer 1968.

A boy watches the work grind on into the night. Autumn 1968.

This man stood in contemplation of the construction for more than one hour without moving. Autumn 1968.

Another transfixed onlooker in a trendy hat and coat of the period. Winter 1968.

To the last of them, the daily pilgrimage of visitors would leave awed by the site's immensity. Winter 1968.

A sewer conduit of unheard-of size. Winter 1968.

Wall Street businessmen. The atmosphere on the street echoed the city's austere economic environment at the time.

Homeless, beneath the Brooklyn Bridge anchorage. Winter 1968.

Catching some rays in winter. 1968.

The promise of the new Trade Center didn't spill over into all sectors. This is Avenue C, home to century-old tenements, many abandoned, like this car turned amusement ride. Winter 1968.

Elsewhere, in old ethnic neighborhoods like Little Italy, a carefree sense of community. Winter 1968.

Intermittently the cold invades, and the presence of life grows sparse. The Towers will split that patch of sky to the south. Winter 1968.

An old couple take a measured evening stroll through snow-blanketed Central Park. Winter 1968.

The low winter sun limns the boundaries where concreteness meets potential. Winter 1968.

Before it became a "destination", Soho was packed with warehouses. Spring 1968.

An older man heads home on the subway. Spring 1969.

Climbing to a Harlem subway stop. Autumn 1968.

"Stop War". The dialogue could not have been more unambiguous at that moment in history.

An antiwar rally on 6th Avenue. Incongruous allies in principle. Autumn 1968.

There was always a demonstration against the war in Vietnam somewhere, every weekend. The participants were from similarly far-flung regions of the political and social landscape. Winter 1968.

You can find anything in New York City, even a white- supremacist fringe. Winter 1968.

Roiling with dissent and economically hard-pressed, the city's atmosphere nonetheless fostered and focused creative energies. Autumn 1968.

Antiwar activists rally in Washington Square. Autumn 1968.

Making a phone call at an antiwar rally in Grand Central Terminal. There were rules of engagement in this conflict, an unspoken understanding of ideals and responsibility. Autumn 1968.

An orthodox Jewish tour group at the Statue of Liberty.

Street performers in Washington Square Park. Summer 1968.

People used to spend their days this way in Washington Square. This park culture flourished unabated for the next two decades. Summer 1968.

The fortress wall at Battery Park didn't hold in the sounds of the World Trade Center being built, just out of sight. Spring 1968.

The noise from the Trade Center site boomed out across the Hudson River piers. Autumn 1968.

A man enjoys a game of *bocce*. Winter 1968.

Bocce strips on East Houston street on the Lower East Side attracted men from all walks. One presumes that many were of Italian descent, but there was no way to know. Winter 1968.

The myriad of life in New York City. Winter 1968.

Bocce on East Houston, from a player's perspective. Winter 1968.

Residents of the Bowery. Autumn 1968.

Differences of bearing, race and uniform, and yet an ineluctable connection that I found compelling and elusive. Veterans on parade. Spring 1968.

A subway train launches for midtown and another emerges from the East River into Queens. Autumn 1968.

Approaching Manhattan from the "mainland" side. Autumn 1968.

Harlem bus riders on Lenox Avenue. Winter 1968.

Light evening traffic heading into Manhattan through the Queens Midtown Tunnel. Autumn 1968.

Gleaming late model cars against an antediluvian backdrop. Autumn 1968.

The village, emblematic of a city embracing discord and passion. Spring 1969.

Dreamtime on the subway. Spring 1969.

The interminable wait for a pizza as antidote to a night of drinking. I'd never tasted pizza until arriving in Manhattan. Spring 1969.

Demolition of old structures continued, even as the new foundation was being excavated. The workplace was a challenging one, and often dangerous.

I was struck by the thought of workmen digging out the Tower's supports with shovels and bare hands. Spring 1968.

Workmen at the base of the huge construction site looked like ants. Spring 1969.

The site demanded a rethinking of architectural proportion, even at this stage. Spring 1969.

Traffic would not slow down while construction marched continuously forward. Spring 1969.

I was mesmerized by the enormity of what humans can create. Spring 1969.

Working on the exterior walls. Finished, they appeared uncannily slender. Here you feel the full weight of their substance. Spring 1969.

Construction proceeds at breakneck speed. Spring 1969.

Conferring, reconnoitering, constant action and assessment. Spring 1969.

A construction site foreman with his next in command. Spring 1969.

A building unlike any I've known takes shape as the steel skeleton grows. Spring 1969.

As the Towers climb inexorably skyward, other structures around them are still coming down.

A gentle counterpoint to the bleakness of the construction zone.

Liberty Street, in front of the proposed South Tower. In the distance another economic pillar, the Federal Reserve Bank. Spring 1969.

I could feel the power of America in this building's construction. Summer 1969.

Steel fingers grasp at the sky as the building continues to materialize. Summer 1969.

It will soar past its stolid elders. Autumn 1969.

At this stage, I still wasn't aware the building would clear 100 stories. Autumn 1969.

I never tired of photographing the construction and people involved. Autumn 1969.

It was at this stage that I first recognized the delicacy of the building's design. Autumn 1969.

Nearly finished, the distinctive antennas had yet to be mounted.

Like the city they dominated, there was a gracefulness that belied the Towers' strength.

New York's polyglot architectural vocabulary on one Village street: From mid-nineteenth century to mid- twentieth. In the distance, the thrust toward a new millennium.

Greenwich Village once seemed worlds away from the working neighborhoods near the southern waterfront.

The revised shoreline of New York Harbor, mid-'80's.

The sun sets on the working world.

A worker at the nearby Fulton Fish Market sees no difference in his workaday world. The old commerce soldiered on in these places. Spring 1969.

A quiet holiday in Harlem. Spring 1969.

Resting at the Metropolitan Museum. Spring 1968.

Waiting for the ferry. Spring 1969.

Amidst a changing city, an oasis of concentration. A game of checkers in the park. Summer 1968.

Height of summer, 1968.

Nuns hurry along Seventh Avenue. Autumn 1968.

A fall evening in Central Park, 1968.

A slight difference of opinion. Spring 1969.

The air of an earlier time refused to depart this downtown boxing gym.

A whole new topography at the end of the island.

A stunning silhouette.

Ground Zero, December 2001

1968

Ground Zero, December 2001

1968

Ground Zero, December 2001

Three months after the attack. December 2001.

A young girl, 1968.

[The World Trade Center Complex]

The World Trade Center, North Tower and South Tower

Chief Architect: Minoru Yamasaki

Architects: Minoru Yamasaki & Associates of Troy, Michigan, and Emery Roth and Sons of New York City.

General Constructor: Tishman Reality and Construction Company of New York City.

Built from 1973.

Constructed of lightweight steel and glass supported by exterior columns.

Height: 110 stories, 1,362 feet (412 meters)

Rentable space of floor area: 10 million square feet

Total cost: 857 million dollars

[Minoru Yamasaki]

Architect, born December 1912, in seattle, Washington, as a second-generation Japanese. Graduated from University of Washington in 1934 by earning his living working at salmon canneries. An enthusiastic educator, many of his pupils are now found around the world. Received the awards from American Institute of Architects(AIA).

1934-45	Received a master's degree from New York University. Worked at several firms as Shreve, Lamb and Harmon, designers of the Empire State Building, amd Harrison, Fouilhoux and Abramovitz, designers of Rockefeller Center.
1945	Moved to Detroit as chief of design for Smith Hinchman & Grylls, a distinguished firm established in 1853.
1949	Left Smith Hinchman & Grylls to form a partnership with fellow architects George Hellmuth and Joseph Leinweber.
1959	Formed his own firm, Minoru Yamasaki & Associates.
1986	Died in February, aged 73.

A partial list of his works :

U.S. Consulate, Kobe, Japan, 1954

Century Plaza Hotel, Los Angeles, 1966

Eastern Airlines Terminal, Logan International Airport, Boston, 1968

World Trade Center Complex, New York, 1977

Miyko Hotel, Tokyo, 1979

Shinji Shumeikai Hall, Shiga, Japan, 1988.

Of the many whose lives were deeply entwined with the fate of the World Trade Center, two distinguished individuals were asked to contribute their thoughts to this book. Leslie E. Robertson, with his firm, is responsible for some of the most significant structural engineering innovations of the past half-century. The indisputable brilliance of his tower structure, built to a standard of excellence far higher than was necessary for it to merely stand, was greatly responsible for saving the majority of lives on September 11th. For Jacqueline Gavagan, a single year contained a lifetime's worth of cataclysm. Yet she confronted her compounded tragedy with clarity of conviction. Her response was a direct and moving repudiation of that day's havoc — a commitment to answering hate with love and death with life.

This book of photographs provides a fascinating perspective into the creativity of a fine photographer...a photographer who, with this collection, has captured insightful moments in the lives of buildings and of people. As the engineer who directed and who bears responsibility for the structural design of the two towers of the World Trade Center, I find myself torn between a preoccupation with the images of the buildings and the images of those persons who might somehow have perished inside of them.

Certainly, you will find a telling story of the World Trade Center as it rose from the negative space of a giant bathtub to soar into the positive space of the sky; indeed, the two towers did so in a way never achieved before or since. Clearly, Hideaki Sato somehow sensed and anticipated the grandness and the power of the finished buildings. Perhaps there was within him a sensory relationship with the Japanese-American architect, Minoru Yamasaki, as well as with my own fascination with, and appreciation of, the architecture and the culture of Japan.

Now, looking back to the time of these photographs of the World Trade Center in the context of 11 September, one cannot help but find a curious juxtaposition in this work of Sato's. That is, the strength of the structures of the World Trade Center is stated in a convincing and profound manner, while at the same time, a kind of melancholy is stamped onto these same structures — a melancholy that may not have been anticipated in the instant of the opening and the closing of the shutter. Only a small part of this melancholy stems from the colorful images residing in my own mind's eye, as they attempt to relate to the black and white images to be found in this book.

Sato-san has provided powerful photographs that may, in a way, assist us in calling forth our own memories of the past, our own overwhelming grief of the present, and our own aspirations for the future. For many of us, perhaps for you, some of the images will bring forth tears, or remembrance of loved ones, and of buildings, which can no longer be experienced by the physical senses. Without question, this book provides a foundation, challenging the mind to seek its own images of that which should replace the World Trade Center...that which will bring honor and distinction to those who perished on 11 September.

As well, for those with a keen eye, this book will lead forward our understanding that those loved ones who perished, that those buildings, are not truly lost...that they will remain forever in our minds, in our hearts and in our daily lives.

Leslie E. Robertson, 01 June 2002

Today, my husband, Donald Gavagan, has a bench named in his memory. It's by the lighthouse near his beloved retreat in Montauk, Long Island. I can sit there and compose my thoughts of him.

In 1998 we had twins together, Lara and Donald III. The path to their birth had been difficult, and they truly seemed a miracle. Shortly after their birth we received shattering news. Our son had a congenital heart defect that required delicate open-heart surgery. We were devastated. Nothing we'd been through had prepared us for this. But the surgery was performed in March of 2001, it was successful, and to multiply the blessing, we soon learned we would have another child.

I was seven months into that pregnancy on September 11th. It was an ordinary, hectic day. The kitchen was being demolished for refurbishing and the dust was awful, so I took the kids outside to play. I had to watch the news from a neighbor's house. I was gripped with fear for Donald, but I'd received a call from his friend suggesting he'd shortly be finding his way out of his office in Tower One. When Tower Two fell, I still had full faith in my husband's strength and quick mind. He was a problem solver, and if there were a way out, he would find it. With the fall of the north tower, I turned to prayer. I prayed that he would see his twins again, and even more, the child still waiting to be born.

The problem presented to Donald that day was too great even for him. He never came home. His life disappeared without a trace. Just a few days later I learned that my new baby would be a boy. Connor was born 52 days after, a brother for Donald, a gift from heaven. I want to believe he is a guardian angel, sent from above.

It's possible that hope is easy to see, but not easy to recognize until you've seen what hopelessness looks like. In the weeks after my husband's death I began to think of the crisis we'd recently faced, and how it seemed to us the worst thing conceivable — our gentle child, having to undergo difficult and possibly painful surgery, with uncertain results. But we had everything we needed to help him. We had health insurance, the best surgical care, we had the means to give him a long and healthy life. We had choices. We had *each other*. We were not helpless. I began to imagine what it would be like to face that tragedy without any of what we had.

It was at that moment that I decided to set up a memorial fund, The Donald Richard Gavagan, Jr. Fund, with Project Kids Worldwide. I was helpless the morning of September 11th and could not save my husband's life. But I could turn the horrible energy of that day completely around to make it a force for the renewal of life. If, through my husband's memory, children's lives can be saved, if the plague of helplessness can be lifted from a parent's shoulders, then something good could come out of this nightmare. The healing of many children's hearts will help mend our own broken hearts. I want my children never to forget their daddy's thoughtfulness, zest for life and generosity.

Jacqueline Gavagan, Spring 2002

If you wish to make a contribution to the memory of Donald Richard Gavagan, Jr., please forward donations to:

Project Kids Worldwide
C/O Cardiac Service Line
New York University Medical Center
Skirball Building, Suite 9Z
530 First Avenue New York, NY 10016
Phone: 212-263-8141
www.projectkidsworldwide.org

Project Kids Worldwide is a charitable organization dedicated to surgical research, innovation and providing life saving open-heart surgery to children in medically underserved areas of the United States and the World.

Donald will be remembered through your gifts. Medical programs, life saving advances and care provided through Project Kids Worldwide will be a tribute to his strong family values and his abiding concern for others.